# A COIN FOR *the* FERRYMAN

by

Katherine Scholfield

Grosvenor House
Publishing Limited

Katherine Scholfield is hereby identified as author of this
work in accordance with Section 77 of the Copyright, Designs
and Patents Act 1988

The book cover picture is copyright to Inmagine Corp LLC

This book is published by
Grosvenor House Publishing Ltd
28-30 High Street, Guildford, Surrey, GU1 3EL.
www.grosvenorhousepublishing.co.uk

A CIP record for this book
is available from the British Library

ISBN 978-1-78148-670-2

For Alice, Dougal, Toby and Lucy

# CONTENTS

# IMAGINE

And the woman took the apple
from the Tree of Knowledge,
thought, for a moment, about giving it to the man
but changed her mind.
Instead she ate it.
She then studied for degrees:
higher mathematics,
philosophy, history and political science.
She changed the world.
Her sons, born after a necessary one-night stand
(no IVF or sperm banks in those days)
grew up in touch with their feminine side
and never fought or started wars.
Her daughters learned to plough.
The human breed flourished,
wise and kind,
compassionate and good,
and John Lennon never had to write
"Imagine."

# THE JUMPER

When he was a boy
he spent the summers by a creek,
just lazing, a fishing rod at his side,
and always a book.
A clever boy,
they said,
he loves his books.
He'll go far.

When it got too hot
he'd jump from the bank
into the pool below.
He'd hold his nose against the surging water
and fall endlessly into darkness,
then would surface again,
laughing,
brushing back his wet hair
and swimming to the side
with easy, life-loving strokes.

He was on the 80th floor
when the first plane hit.
They thought it was an earthquake.
Better get out,
someone said,
but the lift was jammed.
Then fire.

They opened windows and waved to helicopters.
Come and get us,
they said.
It seemed so easy.

When he jumped
he remembered those summer days
and held his nose.

# SLEEPING BEAUTY

By the time he'd hacked through the wood
and she'd slept for a hundred years
they were both old.
Her hair was completely white,
her skin like crumpled tissue paper.
He'd lost most of his teeth and all his hair
and walked with a limp,
one leg shorter than the other,
legacy of a fall from a horse in a long-ago joust.

He stood for a long time looking at her
as the years fell away
and he was filled with yearning
for the princess of his young dreams.
He slipped a Viagra from his tunic,
and felt the sap rise again.

Tenderly he touched her cheek.
She opened her eyes and smiled in welcome,
then pulled him to her on the narrow bed
beside the spinning wheel.

They made love for hours.
Afterwards, he told her his adventures,
and she told him her dreams.

"Will you marry me?" he asked on bended knee,
despite arthritic pain.
"Yes," she whispered.

They lived happily ever after.

# THE MERMAID

When I was a mermaid
I would lie on my back on the seabed
and gaze for hours at the waters above me.
Strange visions I saw:
black-keeled ships which roared and churned
and troubled the waters,
constellations of silvery fishes wheeling and diving;
seaweed drifting like waves in my hair
and the cold whiteness of icebergs
where I could see reflections and images
which moved and shaped and formed.
Of them all, I loved the icebergs best.

A mortal man beguiled me,
and gave me legs
where my shimmering tail had been.
He took me to his world
and let me walk.
At night I wrapped my legs around him
and forgot about the sea.

But sometimes now, when all is quiet,
I lie on my back in the meadow
and watch the white clouds
as they move and shape and form
in the sky above me.
Old memories of reflections and images
roar and churn.
And I am heartsick for icebergs.

# OLD MAN

His eyes are wet with rheum.
He fumbles for the bell with palsied hands,
shouts, "Nurse" or sometimes "Japs,"
then falls asleep
a gob of spittle on his chin.

Once he ran races, climbed mountains,
loved, and lost
and loved again.
Went to war, came back,
married,
raised children, paid off a mortgage,
voted for politicians and ran a small,
but quite successful business
dealing in car parts.

Sometimes he remembers,
but mostly
doesn't.

# DIWALI IN AGRA

Warm night engulfs the city,
lights begin to twinkle
and buildings darken.

I'm on a bus,
weary after the long journey
from Jaipur,
my head falling sleepily
against the window glass.

Then I see her.
A sari-clad woman with two children:
a little girl with lustrous plaits
and a boy,
his hair neatly combed
and a white shirt
gleaming above dark trousers,
grown up but still a child.

She carries a tray of food
lit by candles.
Her walk is purposeful, deliberate,
as she shepherds her children.
They too hold lights.

It is Diwali:
the Festival of Light,
and I watch them
as they walk,
encircled in their own
careful brightness.

Our worlds are momentarily merged
as I watch these rings of light.
I wish she'd catch my eye.

The bus moves on.

# LIFE FLOW

Born where the Murrumbidgee's dark-green waters
meandered through rolling hills in New South Wales,
creating billabongs of memory and dreams of horizons,
swagmen and bunyips and love of distances,
she let other rivers carry her onwards.

First the Thames,
and rainy afternoons of London autumn,
falling leaves a broken refrain
for first loves and ancient yearnings,
answers to a primal call.

Then that Springtime in Paris,
warm sunshine and smell of fresh bread,
coffee roasting in a hundred cafes,
as the Seine saw 1968
flow through her life and into history.

He took her to the Tagus, Rhine,
Tiber, Arno and the Loire
then home to Manhattan's great Hudson,
where they hatched their young
then watched them grow and fly away.

She brought his ashes back
to where the broad sweep of the Murrumbidgee
called her home.

White haired and lined, she sits, letting peace
ripple at her feet.

# GRENDEL'S MOTHER

And was it you who killed the old man
and the young ones?
Did you burn houses and break shop windows,
steal television sets and mobile phones?
You have done well, my son -
you show great promise.
Take my iPhone and plan more mayhem.
They won't be able to touch you.
Post your plans on Facebook and meet your friends
in the market place.
Bring me home a pair of Chanel sunglasses,
Christian Louboutin shoes and a Louis Vuitton holdall
and get us both some Nike trainers
so we'll be fleet of foot.
Beowulf, that old Etonian moraliser,
will be on our trail
trying to make a name for himself.
But I ask you,
what else could be expected?
We're from a sink estate.

# CLEANING SHOES

I'm cleaning a pair of shoes
the old-fashioned way,
using polish that I rub on with a cloth
and then shine with a brush
and elbow grease.
With one hand inside a shoe to hold it steady,
I suddenly remember my father
cleaning my school shoes,
black lace ups with a sturdy sole.
I see his big hand inside one small shoe
and the other one brushing.
The memory burns
and leads to another,
of when my mother was in hospital
with a newborn baby.
Dad prepared my school lunch,
a home-made pasty, clumsy and misshapen
and wrapped it in brown paper.
It must have fallen from my bag
as I played my nine year old's games
because, at morning assembly,
it was held up by a teacher
to be reclaimed.
"Somebody's lunch," he shouted,
examining it quizzically.
"Looks like....I don't really know..."
his voice trailed away, sniggering.

As the titters broke out I stood silent,
embarrassed and ashamed
of my father.

Now I am ashamed
of my cowardice.

# AN OLD WOMAN REMEMBERS HER HORSES

She stirs, fretful, in torpid half-slumber
as slow afternoon segues into dusk,
in a chair at St. Raphael's Residential Home.
Around her is scattered evidence of too long a life:
a walking frame, a commode, a bag of incontinence pads
and, on the dresser, some photographs of the family
who come to visit only to sit in embarrassed silence
and offer platitudes or talk about the weather.

Then, in dream or daze, she hears their hoof beats,
faint at first,
but insistent as memory of drumming rain
on roof slates of childhood.
Closer she hears them, thundering now,
like the crashing waves they race beside;
and then she sees them:
foam-flecked they gallop boldly down the strand,
with flowing manes and tails like sunlit waterfalls.

"Ah, my beauties", she croons, in the voice they know.
"Come to me, my lovelies,
Come, come - Sheherazade, Sinead, and Captain Moonlight."
The horses stop and turn, surprised at their old names,
then trot towards her, submissive as children.
They reach her side to whinny and nuzzle about her
as she stands, proudly, a captured princess,
owner and owned.

Sheherezade, the swift Arabian
soothes her with her breath as the old woman murmurs,
"Remember how we won the prize - the blue rosette -
at the county show, the year my son was born?"
She leans into the muscled neck, and feels power,
tempered by the willing obedience of love.
"Sinead, my little Irish mare, my dark colleen, my darling,
remember the cross-country course where we outran them all
through ditches and drops and water, jumping like deer?"
The dark mare bows her head
and leans into the hand that grooms her neck
gentle as a mother.
"And Captain Moonlight, my bold grey hunter,
how fearlessly we rode to hounds, taking fences like flight,
following the pack as they ran up the fell
in the cold bright light of a winter's morning,
with steam rising from horses
and the Master's horn blowing clear and loud."
The big grey stands quietly, his soft eyes closed,
as though in thought or prayer.

"Take me with you," she begs,
to where you live, in Paradise.
My body is a burden:
my legs, once strong to urge you,
are frail, like broken twigs;
my back is bent and twisted
and my hands would never hold a rein."

They turn and race away, three horses,
red and black and grey.
But in the evening, when the nurses come,
they find her dead, her face a radiance of calm.

"She has gone home," they say,
then draw the curtains and strip the bed.

# ON READING HENRY KENDALL'S "THE LAST OF HIS TRIBE"

The old school-house, full of broken memories
like violin chords
played on a rusty instrument,
stands empty and alone.
Ghost children -
girls in gingham dresses and boys in rough boots
who learned their lessons here
years ago-
inhabit corners and sing in chimneys.

The books lie scattered, yellow-paged,
heavy with dust of neglect
and the musty weight of decades,
among insects
harried by the wind
which has blown chaff under warped doors
and through broken windows.

I take one and open it.
And read.
And read again.
I am ten years old.

More than fifty summers on,
I still remember
heat and dust,
the smell of pepper trees,
and a white child's feelings of sadness
for the one black man
left behind.

# MONARCH BUTTERFLIES
# IN MEXICO

We tied our horses
and let them graze,
then hiked a while, and suddenly
came into an open glade.

The breeze blew,
or so we thought;
until we realized
the day was windless.

The leaves had turned;
or so we thought,
until we realised
the trees were evergreen.

Monarch Butterflies in their thousands
hung in the branches,
a drowsy fluttering of wings
heralding day.

We waited, spellbound
as the sun rose
and trees became alive
as the butterflies took flight.

They filled the earth and sky:
circling, wheeling, mating,
resting, and sometimes even dying
at our feet.

Each year, driven by an ancient call,
fed on slender milkweed,
they journey to this place,
to spend warm winters in Mexico.

And then, compelled again by instinct
the perilous journey north
to far-off Canada begins,
and they go home again.

# A POEM FOR OSCAR

The photos come by internet from half the world away:
a tiny, newborn human child,
lies squashed and squalling, red faced,
on his mother's chest.
She lies back, exhausted, elated,
suffused with new-found mother-love
which would kill for, die for, the scrap she holds,
vulnerable as happiness,
tenacious as love,
precious as joy.

We look for hopeful similarities – his father's eyes,
cleft chin and pouting lip from his mother's genes.
They sleep. He learns to feed,
sneezes, sucks his thumb,
cries, and is comforted.
This most mundane of miracles
binds us to one another,
and reaches out
everywhere.

For him the conductor's baton is raised
to start the sweetest music.
The scientist searches anew
for undiscovered worlds
and the philosopher finds truths.

For him the cat licks her kittens
then carries them to safety,
the vixen tends her young
in warm lair-darkness.
A nursing whale suckles her young,
and a crocodile's egg is hatched.

And for this moment,
infinite and intimate,
evanescent and eternal,
we touch the stars, and understand
everything.

# WAR AND PEACE

Cold clear dawn when the squadron's scrambled,
and the boy-men, stumbling from their cots,
pull on their flying-suits, fingers all a-fumble.
"We'll really give them what-for, lads," he says,
their boy commander, his clear eyes bright for battle.

The engines roar like surf,
the runway drops away.
They climb towards the orb of waking sun -
the sea below gleams pewter pale.
They fly as in their dreams,
the hum of engines lulling them,
like girls' soft hands and lilting voices.
Then, "Flak! Flak!
Watch it, Jimmy,"
"Steady as she goes.
We're doing well.
Good work, lads.
We're over target now."

So it's Bombs Away and turn to face the west.
The boys exult, joyful in ancient comradeship
of men and war.
They laugh, and talk of girls and beer:
they're going home.

But then: "We're hit! We're hit! We're losing oil."
The engine coughs: fear catches in their throats.
"D'you think we'll make it, sir?"
"It's OK, lads, of course we will.
We'll glide her home from here."
(Unless, he doesn't say, she catches fire.)

And so they travel, each one strangely silent
with thoughts of death, until they start to sing
and make it home.

Now he sits in twilight, old man with memories
of Jack, and Bill, and Ken, and red-haired Martha,
who once was briefly loved, in the way of war.
Now Nurse Jackson rubs his swollen feet
with soothing cream, then helps him with his slippers.
"What's for tea?, he quavers, peevishly.
"Cauliflower cheese," she says. "Your favourite."
She pats him absentmindedly, before she moves away.

Wearily, he shuts his eyes, and dreams once more
of going home.

# THE OLIVE GROVE

Thirty years ago,
when their children were small
they planted an olive grove:
four hundred trees,
fragile and vulnerable, like the children,
with hopeful lives in root and leaf:
they tended and watered them
til they, too, grew strong.

Twenty years ago
their first harvest yielded
thirty litres of oil -
the best they'd ever tasted,
they all agreed, as the green liquid
caught the light.
And they were simply, ordinarily happy.

The children left,
everyone grew older;
the farm was sold
for other plans
and they scattered themselves
to winds and oceans.

Now, thirty years later,
they came back
on a whim,
just to drive the old familiar road
and look across the fence
into a farm
with someone else's name
on the gate.

Somehow it didn't matter about the name
that wasn't theirs,
or that the house had changed:
the farm was still there,
flourishing, as in their yesterdays.
Willows still grew by the river
and grass was lush on the hillside.

And in the distance they could see
the olive grove,
alive and fruitful,
a proud, dark shape
against the summer sky.

# LINES WRITTEN FOR
# A POETRY TUTOR

## -and for Dylan Thomas,
## Ezra Pound and W H Auden

When, like Dylan, I feel "the slow boiling in the belly of
a bad poem"
and take my pen in hand,
I stop to spare a thought for Alison,
who has to read it.
Through all my infelicitous phrasing and sloppy punctuation,
my unclear thought and second hand emotion
I wonder if there ever shines, for just a moment
the pure light of Erato,
or if, like Mauberley
I have been "wrong from the start"
to try to "resuscitate the dead art of poetry"
with such poor and misbegotten arrows in my quiver.

How did they do it, the old masters?
How is it that "about suffering they were never wrong?"
Did they feel it in their bones
or was it simply lucid observation,
external and remote?
Where did the words come from:
a source within, or from a distant creator who loves not me?
Or from such love, or joy, or hope,
despair or pain, or even hate
so strong I cannot know it,

even less describe it?
Do I, too, write to save the broken statues
and battered books of civilization
or merely to indulge a whim?

Is it worth it?

I pick up my pen
and try again.

# HALLOWEEN HOUSEWIFE

I take my broomstick
while my wild black cat
shrieks and rages.
My nails grow long,
my teeth pointed
and my hair matted.

Today I used my inoffensive broom
to sweep the kitchen floor,
while my tame cat purred contentedly
in my tidy kitchen
where I live my tidy, inoffensive life.

But all changes when the Old Ones call:
when graves open
and rotting ghouls
begin to walk.
I feel tingling in my skin
and know I must reply.

Invisibly I fly around the village,
creating mayhem:
hens refuse to lay,
cows to give milk,
children become disobedient,
wives won't have sex
and men grow sullen and silent.

I cast my spells widely:
birthmarks on babies,
hunches on backs,
warts on noses.
What fun! I croak
as I swoop and dive,
scattering children
as they trick and treat.

On Halloween I am transformed,
til daybreak dawns
and I go back
to ordinary housewifery.
But every now and then,
when the wind howls,
my cat looks across at me.
And I swear I see her wink.

# SHE PAINTS HER
# TOENAILS RED

She undressed behind the screen.
You could hear the careful way
she folded her clothes
and placed them on the chair.
You held her arm as you helped her climb
onto the consulting couch,
sisterly more than doctor.
You tried to keep your face a mask
as you felt the solid mass
growing inside her:
no child this, no joy,
no happy ending;
nothing but death,
and she knew too.
But you smiled at her
as you saw the defiant scarlet paint
on her toenails.
"I love the colour."
"Yes," she said,
"I thought it would be nice
for the summer.
When I get a tan."

# A SONG FOR
# THE WORKING MAN

I'm on a Greyhound bus:
Connecticut to New York
after a visit to Yale, the university campus
where ancient walls reflect light of privilege,
wealth,
and confidence.

Our driver is hunched over the wheel,
his feet on the pedals.
His socks, showing above worn black shoes
have stitched on them
a red Greyhound logo.

And I am moved, as if to tears.

I hope he wears them proudly
and that his wife launders them with care.
I hope he has a sense of pride, and dignity
and that he feels worthwhile
as he ferries strangers from town to town.

I hope his employer
treats him fairly,
pays him well,
and praises his good work
when he gives him a Christmas bonus.

I hope he doesn't mind
not being a doctor
or a teacher
or a scientist.

And I hope that they
don't act superior,
and that they thank him
when they get off the bus.

# ME AND ANDY MURRAY

I can't bear it,
watching the tennis,
unless I don't care who wins
and then I usually stop watching
because I don't care who wins.

But I wanted Andy to win
ever since I heard
he was at Dunblane:
eight years old
walking towards the gym
when the shots rang out.
He says he doesn't remember
but I do.
I was nearly fifty.

I couldn't bear to watch a match
until I knew he'd won,
then viewed the replay
and cheered him on.
But soon I knew
that to be a fan and help him win
I needed to watch it live
to give support.

I tried.

I couldn't.

To me he was still eight years old
and didn't understand
how cruel life can be
and how unfair.

I prayed one year he'd make it
and win a Slam.
Then I could forget Dunblane
and the little boy
walking towards the gym.
And I would watch
every match.

**Coda: 2013**

And he did.
And so I can.

# THE LAST LIVING THING I SHOT

The last living thing I shot
was a rabbit,
a terrible pest
which ate my father's grass
and undermined the fields.

I took aim with my shotgun,
a twelve bore.
I saw the feeding rabbit in my sights
and fired.
It was a clean kill.

I walked to where my trophy lay,
a doe, still warm.
I saw the red stain
darkening her fur
and her eyes glaze blankly.

A thing that once had life,
ran heedlessly, burrowed,
mated, and fed its young,
now was dead:
and at my hand.

I have no love for rabbits
but on that day
I vowed never again to aim to kill
another living thing.

# SHAKESPEARE'S LAMENT

What a piece of work
is man – or woman for that matter.

Signing on for the dole and complaining
that it isn't enough
and that the government should tax the rich more.
Wasting time in doctors' surgeries
with complaints that would get better
by themselves,
given a few days;
demanding antibiotics
and a sick note.

Binge drinking on the weekends
and vomiting outside pubs
and in taxis
and getting into fights
with strangers.

Littering beauty spots
with crisp wrappers and drinks cans
and dogshit they put in plastic bags
then hang in trees
for someone else
to deal with.

Voting for the party who offers the most
bread and circuses
then turning against them
when they don't perform miracles.

Coupling for lust and breeding
for benefits,
entertained by reality television
and fattened by junk –

what is this quintessence of dust?

# BRUMBY STALLION

High Country, NSW/Victoria Border

The wild black colt,
exultant in his liberty,
gallops towards us, head held high.

I stand to watch,
my old bay mare obedient to the bit
and leg and voice of human.

He calls,
the ancient, atavistic cry.
She trembles under my weight.

Come with me, love,
he calls: come away, away,
away from hands that bind.

He circles nearer,
calls her again,
sniffing her scent in the air.

"Walk on", I say
and my mare obeys.
And he runs back to freedom.

# CAFE SOCIETY BUENOS AIRES

Sitting in a cafe
in Buenos Aires
we talk about how pleasant
life is here.

The city dwellers
for whom this place is home
are urbane, elegant
helpful and polite.
They smile at strangers
and point the way
to Eva Peron's tomb
in Recoleta Cemetery.

Forty years ago
in the Dirty War,
students were dragged from homes
at night
and tortured to death,
their weighted bodies
dropped from aeroplanes
into the Rio Plata,
to sink from memory;
memory miraculously salvaged
and kept alive by mothers
in Plaza Mayo.

Who did these things?
The smiling couple on the left?

The helpful waiter?
The florist?
A crucible of evil
lurks at the heart of every human;
even ours, dear friend.

We order another coffee,
And fresh orange juice.

# AUBADE

Her son flies to Philadelphia,
his sister catches the Tube to work
then cycles at weekends
down Whitehall.
Her grandson sleeps,
alone in his cot, his nursery
twelve thousand miles away.

First light and birdsong;
Radio Four segues into consciousness.

The cafe in Marrakech, where she lunched last year,
has been bombed,
paedophiles are on the loose,
Republicans might yet
make Donald Trump a President.
Oh help.

Warfare, wickedness and murder,
even walking downstairs
or catching a bus
is filled with hazard.
A step the wrong way here,
a slip there, a careless driver
a faulty switch, human evil.
Oh help!

Keep my little ones safe,
she pleads to the morning.
For the world is filled with peril
and they are small, so fragile
in such a cosmos
which neither know or cares
how much she loves,
how little she can do.

She gets up, makes tea,
then telephones.
Everyone is well, and happy.
She sighs relief.
Until tomorrow's dawn.

# OUT WITH OSCAR

The first time I took Oscar to the park
on my own
I was quite unnerved,
although he didn't seem to notice.
Strapped in his pushchair,
he seemed blithely unconcerned,
joyful even,
as we set off down the hill
with the brake off,
avoiding the traffic
and keeping an anxious lookout
for child molesters.

We saw a dog.
"Dog," he said,
then "woof."
"That's right," I said,
"you clever boy,"
as though he'd split the atom.

We saw a little girl.
"Wave to her," I said,
"she's smiling."
He waved, and she waved back.
Her mother didn't seem to notice
my inexperience
and she smiled too.

We reached the park -
a carnival alive with mums and little ones
and dads and grannies,
among the swings and seesaws.
A hum of chatter, squeals and laughter
was background to this smaller world
of children's knowing.

I needed help
to unfasten the childproof pushchair belt
as Oscar struggled.
"Both sides," they said, "at once."
The mums, smug in their special knowledge,
smiled indulgently.
It clicked
and he was free.

We watched the ducks
and played on swings.
"Be careful.
You're too little for that one -
that one's for bigger boys."
(Oh, responsibility!)
And then he cried,
but only briefly.
"Look, here's a biscuit."
My powers to comfort grew.

A granny from Turkey
became my passing friend
as Theo played with Oscar on the climbing frame

until they both got tired.
"Goodbye," we said
and then walked home
to wait for Daddy.

Again,
miraculously spared from speeding cars,
paedophiles
and my lapses of attention,
he was asleep when we reached the door.

# WOVEN MEMORIES

Before I left for boarding school,
I remember seeing my mother
bent over her sewing
stitching name tags
onto all my clothes:
Cash's Woven Names,
they were called.
They came in a long strip
that was cut into lengths
with my name in blue letters
in capitals.
I remember her small, neat stitching
on my tunics, gym slips
socks and knickers,
with such painstaking
as only mothers know.

Fifty years later I again watched her,
bent with age,
sewing name tags onto my father's clothes
to take into the nursing home.
I saw the same small, careful stitches
and the neat knots
and heard the snip of the scissors
cutting the strands of her life.

I am humbled by her love.

# THE GIFT

And who is this,
on a cold night in November,
bringing sudden warmth
and slow rekindling of an old hunger
in the desert of age?

A glance which lingers,
a hand brushing mine.
Perhaps an accident?
But then we navigate together,
our separate compasses
miraculously synchronised.

And then, ah then
we warm the night with body heat
and words, lit true by moonlight,
eternal in the evanescence
of shy, shared tenderness of strangers.

And so the morning:
strange silences, discomfited goodbyes.
Will you remember from time to time
and feel a moment's gladness?
I will believe it so.

It's now December.

# LONDON 2012

We knew it wouldn't last:
within a week we'd go back to watching
mediocrities on television;
making excuses for the obese,
the feckless, the workshy;
to party-political wrangling
over trivia,
to complaining about public transport,
about interest rates and taxes
and immigration.

But for two weeks we were transfixed:
nothing mattered except
the athletes –
young and talented and proud,
who ran and swam and cycled,
rowed and rode
into history.

Fans draped in flags,
officials with IDs on coloured lanyards
thronged the streets of London;
volunteers helped the lost,
bewildered and the merely curious.
We were polite to one another, we cheered,
we waved, we sang.

Everyone, it seemed, was happy
for two whole weeks.

# SCROVENGI CHAPEL, PADUA

We pass through an airlock chamber
before they let us in
to see the Heavenly Host,
not wanting too much human stain
to spoil the fragile paint.
But Giotto's frescoes,
as bright and pure
as in the quattrocento,
make us hold our breath
and stand transfixed in wonder.
Angels swoop and dive
like swallows
in skies of infinite blue
where death's defeated
and the virgin smiles.
Her little child is born:-
the baby come to save the world.

Our world's not saved.

Outside in Padua's streets
we buy espressos at a coffee bar,
then I select a pair of shoes, bright red,
in a shop full of coloured choices.
We catch a train back to Venice
breathing afternoon air
of city, smoke and tired canal.

And wonder why.

# THERE'S SOMETHING
# ABOUT LIFE

When I was a little girl
we lived on a farm,
with sheep, cows and horses
and cats to catch mice.

With no vets for miles
and not much money either,
newborn kittens
were simply drowned.

My grandfather would weigh
a hessian sack with stones,
put the kittens in and tie a knot,
then throw them in the creek.

One day, alone, I watched and waited
after grandfather had gone
and saw the bag burst open:
six mewing kittens,
wet-furred and terrified,
struggled for the shore.

Unobserved,
I helped them onto dry land,
and watched as they blindly crawled
in panic, to nowhere in particular.

Maybe they died there that night,
maybe a fox or crow ate them.
But I always hoped their mother found,
and fed and warmed and comforted them.

If they'd lived and grown
they'd have become a pest:
feral cats,
killing ground-nesting birds
and even our ducklings.

I knew I did wrong
but, looking back,
I don't regret it.

There's something about life...

# TWELFTH NIGHT

And so, once more,
as in all the other years
that I remember,
the Christmas tree is taken down
and the decorations, lovingly collected
over the years,
are stowed away.
The fragile angel's wings
are folded in around her golden gown;
and the little toy horse,
his tinkling harness laid flat,
will sleep another year in the dark.
The jewelled egg, stars, bells,
a bird of paradise and the tin soldier,
all are wrapped in tissue paper
and laid gently down.

All memories of childhood,
my own, and others,
are put away with these simple treasures;
each trinket precious as gold
or frankincense,
all tinged with loss,
bitter as myrrh.

Outside, hard, insistent buds
push through the bark on leafless trees.
Although the frost stands hard and bright
and nights still cold as death,
spring will surely come around
and birth will follow.

And so
each year,
the ritual is more poignant,
more full of painful sweetness,
and so,
even more sublime.

# OLD WOMEN

I love old women,
love their lined faces and gnarled hands,
their sagging stockings and sensible shoes.

I love the way they carefully apply
a touch of lipstick
and a dab of cologne.

I like old men too
only they don't smell
as nice.

# SEVEN SINS

Those guilty of gluttony and sloth
are now called victims of a syndrome -
not obese -
and are rewarded with television appearances,
fat camps, and gastric banding
at taxpayers' expense.

The lustful are treated for sex addiction
and make their fortunes
writing books
to feed the appetites of others.

The greedy are fed
with seven figure salaries
and bonuses to match,
own private jets and trophy wives
and flaunt designer children
to the world.

The envious go looting
in riots which set towns ablaze,
and blame social deprivation
and inequality, not sin,
and therefore justified.

The proud and wrathful
take their place in governments
and churches
where they can control
the lowlier lives of others.

The gods look on, bemused,
then sit back
and plan revenge.

# A CASHMERE SWEATER

I brought a gift to take to my father
in the nursing home:
a sweater, blue Argyll,
because he had complained of the cold.

"Cashmere, ma'am, or lambswool?"
the shop assistant had asked.
I chose lambswool,
thinking cashmere a waste
at such a time.

My father thanked me
and, in a moment of rare lucidity,
stroked the sweater.
"Lambswool," he said,
"so soft."

Stung by his gratitude
I regretted not buying
cashmere.

# A CAN OF SHAVING FOAM

After the operation,
when they closed you up again
because they couldn't do anything
she went to visit you in hospital.
You were lying in bed
and she knew that they'd told you the truth
because of your eyes and the bewilderment there.

You clung to one another then talked of tomorrow,
as though it was assured.

On the shelf stood a can of shaving foam,
an unexceptional aerosol,
beside the books and get well cards,
next to the TV remote
and the clock which measured out your minutes.
Defiant and upright, it made its statement:
I am life, it said,
ordinary life.
With my foam the razor will be eased over skin
where beard still grows daily,
along with hair and fingernails,
and heart beating strong.

I smell of good things
and I remind you both of home,
buying groceries, unpacking the car;
the kitchen, the garden
and each small everyday happiness.
As long as I am needed
he will live,
it seemed to say to her.

And she believed.

After you died she took your things home.
The can of shaving foam silently mocked her.

# FROM THE SOMME TO SANGIN

**"Quick March!"**
They look over their shoulders, these ghostly soldiers,
then fade from view down the long lens of history
a hundred years past.

**"Quick March!"**
There were rats in the trenches on the Somme,
lice got into seams of the uniforms
and mud filled men's dreams.
But it would all be over by Christmas,
and this was the war to end all wars.
A boy from Aldeburgh, and one from Hamburg,
go over the top and run towards the wire,
then fade.

**"Quick March!"**
On Normandy beaches Americans joined in
to save the Allies from the monster
who shot himself in a Berlin bunker:
the whole world rejoiced.
But in the cemeteries
rows of crosses silently rebuke
those of us left living.
A farm boy from Nebraska smiles a wistful smile,
then fades.

**"Quick March!"**
Leeches in Vietnam sucked what blood was left
from young men

who were asked to kill other young men
to save the world from one thing or another.
They shot and bombed and bayoneted each other
for years. And then went home.
A South Australian waves to camera,
while a Viet Cong soldier writes love poetry
to his sweetheart,
then fades.

"Quick March!"
In Sangin,
Afghan dust blinds the patrol
as the IED explodes:
four NATO soldiers killed.
Meanwhile, as civilian casualties mount,
mothers and children weep despairing tears
while the enemy holds fast.
The film crew catch the moment
and broadcast to plasma screens in Aberdeen
and Pittsburgh, Sydney and Saigon.
They scan the scene with weary lens,
then fade.

Somewhere, today, a child is born.
Ghostly soldiers crowd around the cradle,
with kindly gestures, and with love
brought back from death.
We would give our lives again, they say,
if only he would never hear the words:
"Quick March!"

They fall in line
and fade away.

# A CRICKET

A cricket landed on my book today
as I lay reading
in my summer garden,
all alive with bee and bird song.
I moved to brush the insect off,
but something made me stop
and watch this creature from the air,
as we inhabited a moment of shared space.

First, it rubbed its legs together
then cleaned its face
with slow, deliberate strokes.
I almost laughed out loud.
It looked at me intently,
its sad, bulbous eyes
inscrutably alien.

We sat a while, the cricket and me,
Trying to fathom each other's separate mysteries.
Did we succeed?

Later,
I heard it singing.

# TOWARDS ENTROPY

There are cobwebs in corners
and dust on shelves.
The leaking roof fills buckets
and cracks in the ceiling
grow wider each year.

Your hands are aching
and you can't bend your knees
without crying out.
You can no longer lift
the coal sacks,
and climbing stairs
gets harder every time.

Sometimes you see yourself
in a mirror,
or reflected in the glass
of a shop window,
and you wonder
who the old woman is.

Then you think of how it all
breaks down, with time:
yourself, your house,
the possessions garnered
lovingly and covetously
in your youth.

And now,
now it all slides
towards chaos,
all going back to where
it came from.

# CHRISTMAS EVE 2009

Christmas Eve,
and she's finished the last
of the 12 kilogram bag of rice
she'd bought ten years earlier
in case the Millenium Bug
closed shops,
stopped the trains
and made aeroplanes fall from the sky.

She takes out her albums,
photos from a dead decade,
and skims through,
wistful, smiling.

Age has taken hold.
Death has scythed his way
into rich pastures of friendships
and left her world diminished.

But birth has mitigated.

"My children, and their children,"
she sighs contentedly
then checks the time.
"They'll soon be here," she says.

She turns on the fairy lights
around the tree
and listens for the car.

# FAMILY WEDDING

She gazes at her son,
so happy in love,
on the cusp of future.
She celebrates,
seeing that beloved child
she bore and fed
and read stories to,
about to take his own place
in the giant scheme.
Her joy brims over:
so why is her heart so sore?

Is it the fragility
of youthful dreams
seen from age,
or fear of danger in a world
where crime and cruelty stalk?
She wants to protect them,
nurture them,
and care for them forever.

She wants their children
to be born in peace
and health,
their jobs secure
and their debts paid off quickly.
She wants them to stay in love,
to share books

and enjoy holidays in sunny places,
to feel sand between their toes
and watch sunsets and sunrises,
and be entranced by nature.
She wants them to be filled with hope:
she wants them to look back
with delight.

Her joy brims over,
piercing like pain.

# FOETAL SCAN

You showed me the photo:
"Here is our baby", you said, proudly,
and together we marvelled
at the grainy black and white image
swirling into your lives.

I recalled another photo, also black and white,
of a galaxy,
in a book by Stephen Hawking,
It is, he tells us,
what our galaxy might look like
from a place far away.

And I felt a chill of fear
for the infinite possibilities
in your small womb-world,
and the vast and terrifying cosmos,
the swing and sway of eternal universe
and the forming child,
inchoate, full of mystery;
perilous as life,
deep as love.

You let me touch your belly
and, as I felt the flutter of your baby's kick,
the universe, familiar and frightening,
expanded under my hand.

# A PRAYER FOR THE AGE

Once in Dresden
fire fell from the skies and madness raged
through a night of horror beyond imagining.
Now the stories and pictures tell
of bodies, twisted and hideous,
burned nameless, lying in molten streets
where babies died in mother's arms,
air sucked from infant lungs as hope expired
in keening agony and helpless grief.

Children tucked in bed,
brides with grooms,
old, young,
sick, well,
sane, mad:
none was spared except by accident,
as if the gods themselves had turned on men
to bring them down.

Now in Dresden flowers bloom.
Two friends sit together in a pleasant square,
drinking coffee and laughing to think
their fathers were once the other's enemy.
Fresh-faced mothers wheel prams
across the cobblestones past Frauenkirche,
the steeple cross designed by an Englishman,
a gift from the people of Coventry.

A tear burns and chokes.

We touch hands, my German friend and I.
Inside the church Russian schoolgirls sing Beethoven
as we sit and muse the paradox
of goodness and nobility
as well as evil in our hearts.
Our eyes are wet as music swells and soars.

"Let mothers run the world," we say,
"and put an end to war."
Imagine no more Dresdens, Guernicas, Hiroshimas,
no more Vietnams, Iraqs, Afghanistans.
Young men, all their mother's sons,
would grow up tall and strong and proud
to till fields,
write books
and make ploughshares
from swords.

# AN ATHEIST VISITS
# A VILLAGE CHURCH

We enter as Maisie thumps out "Sheep May Safely Graze".
She's been the organist for 70 years
and still plays well,
if over-enthusiastically,
with all the stops out.
Nothing to be gained by being fainthearted
at heaven's door.

We take our places in the well-worn pews,
some shuffling, like George,
a Battle of Britain pilot, now almost blind;
led by his faithful wife, Penelope,
who waited for him to return
when they were young.

We rifle through the hymn books
to see if we know them before we start.
I like the old ones I remember from school.
I mark the page for Holy Communion
and am glad it's the Book of Common Prayer,
the sweet Anglican liturgy of my own believing years.

A baby cries, restless in his mother's arms.
"Shhh!" she soothes,
and the wooden seat creaks as she rocks
the rock of ages.
We look around and smile
as a beam of light shines
through a stained-glass window,
blessing her and her child;
or so we would have it.

I wonder what a god would think of us,
this little band of saints and sinners:
young and old, sick and well,
sometimes good and sometimes bad?
I kneel at the altar rail beside my friend,
a gay man - and me an unbeliever.
We raise our cupped hands.

I wonder if God minds us?

# COLONOSCOPY

Here in an alien world
the aquatic ballet of my viscera
dances.
Fern fronds and snaking trails
through which the probe travels
can be seen on the monitor
above me.
I am transfixed.

Green-robed, masked forms
sway in the dizzy jumble of lights,
and the low hum of voices
soothe and calm me.
Narcotic fed I lie
not asleep
yet neither quite awake.

There is art and beauty here
amid the steel of science.
My fragile humanity,
which a cancer would kill,
has its own poetry,
and on the radio, somewhere,
a lark ascends.

Oblivion takes me
to another room.
There, I feel a gentle hand on mine
as a healing voice murmurs
"All clear."
I turn and sleep,
briefly blessed.

# WEDDING MARCH

Veiled and dressed in virgin white,
carrying lilies and prayer book;
in new satin shoes
she steps forward on her father's arm
down the long aisle,
beside the flower decked pews
as the music swells.
Guests turn to watch the bride approach.
Then she begins to scream.

Her mouth becomes
a hideous O
brightened with dental fillings.
Her palate vibrates,
red with strain
and spittle sprays wide.

She writhes and moans
and tries to run
despite bridesmaids' pleading.

The saints above look on, aghast,
at the mayhem in the nave –
the torn and ruined wedding dress,
the flowers limp in her hand.

Her mother faints,
her father shouts at her,
some guests begin to pray
or look away embarrassedly
and whisper to one another other.

The bridegroom at the altar rail
doesn't look unhappy
but merely bemused
as though he'd always expected
something like this.

She'd had this dream
since teenage years
each time a young man called.
At 35 she knew the cause
and decided against marriage.

# PARALLEL UNIVERSE

Coaches arrive, windows tinted dark.
Is it, perhaps, a cricket team
or rock band, passers-by wonder.
People wait on a pavement: ordinary people -
wives and sweethearts, mothers, babies
and proud old fathers who smile and tremble,
as we watch at home on TV.

Ordinary people, waiting.
A child frets and stirs
as coach doors swing open
and cheers rise for the Grenadier Guards,
home from Afghanistan.
Swiftly they rush to embrace,
and tears, long held, flow freely.
Our boys are safe, the women say,
as we watch at home on TV.

Cut to Helmand Province.
Dust and desert,
blood and sand blur lenses
as soldiers talk to camera,
with tales of comradeship and courage,
buoyed up by memories
and bedside photographs,
pride in honest work
and hope for better days,
as we watch at home on TV.

At the rehabilitation hospital
a legless officer exercises,
then fits prostheses, his youth forsworn.
It was worth it all,
he says, with steadfast eye,
I played my part and did my best,
served god and man,
my country and my Queen.
A physiotherapist helps him
as he stumbles,
as we watch at home on TV.

Trooping the colour, the Grenadier Guards,
home, for a time,
from Afghanistan,
march in splendid step
before the ageing monarch.
The officer on horseback reins back,
raising a bright sword
as gun carriages roll,
massed bands play boldly
and the crowds hurrah
and wave a nation's flags,
as we watch at home on TV.

# A ROSE IN TURKEY

I rode a horse through Cappadocia,
across open plains
and over jagged mountains,
sometimes through villages.

The houses were simple,
small plots of land were tilled:
vegetables grown to feed the family,
sometimes some chickens scratched the dirt
or a goat stood tethered.

But one day,
among the rows of beans and cabbages,
I saw, by the door of the house,
a rosebush, on it a single bloom:
a pink rose, defiant and lovely.

I imagined a woman,
aged with care and woe,
remembering to water the rose each day:
a small act of love,
a sense of beauty.

I have a pink rose in my garden
that reminds me.

# HUMMINGBIRDS
# IN NEW MEXICO

Some years ago
I stood, at dusk,
in a garden in New Mexico
up near the Arizona border,
beyond the Badlands,
away along Route 66.

Night was coming down,
the cliffs shone gold and purple,
as the desert's ancient heart
bid farewell
and the sun went away til morning.

My friend brought a container
of sugared water,
and sat it on the table.
I stood close by
and watched and waited.

Soon, I felt them
on the dry, electric air
before I heard or saw them;
ten thousand thousand vibrations
of hummingbirds' wings.

I closed my eyes
and, unafraid,
let them fly around me.
Sometimes they were so close
they touched my hair
like a lover's breath,
gentle and insistent.

They drank their fill
hovering over the container,
the whirr of wings unceasing around me
until the nectar was all gone,
and they flew away.

Later that evening
we lay in the hot-tub
and looked at the stars,
content,
knowing that the hummingbirds
would make it through the night.

# ET IN ARCADIA EGO

Somewhere, in London dark,
a low rumble comes from a train
on the Circle Line,
emerging briefly from underground.
The vibrations shake my walls:
one already scarred with a jagged crack,
the legacy of bombs my whole lifetime ago,
which won't stay mended.
I'm quite fond of it.
"This happened in the Blitz",
I tell my friends
who visit.
I share its pride,
its badge of honour,
for having stood steadfast
in face of enemy action.

The late-night tube runs on,
past Gloucester Road
to Paddington via High Street Kensington
and then beyond, eastbound, and so around again.
All her passengers Minding The Gap
and their own business,
avoiding eye contact
with others in the swaying cars,
lit bright for safety's sake.
Where do they go, I wonder,
at this dark hour,
and the rain falling?

In the burrow of my bedroom,
cosily cocooned beneath street-level,
I watch TV news with the volume low,
one ear primed for a longed-for sound.
A mug of cocoa beside me
and a cat curled up,
asleep,
twitching in her dreams.
Her body-heat warms me
through the duvet,
like a hot-water bottle
against my thigh.
I lie still so as not to wake her.

Then, outside, a black cab
purrs into the street,
and shudders into silence at my door.
I hear voices and doors slammed shut:
the taxi hums away.
Keys jingle in the lock,
feet thud softly on carpeted stairs.
Jacket, tie and briefcase are abandoned
as you lean to kiss me, home at last.

Now you are in my arms, my love,
and this is paradise.

# SEASONS: FOR TOM

He left us in Springtime:
the sheep heavy in wool
and paddocks green and lush,
swollen with crops he'd sown
but would not harvest.

We talked of ordinary things:
the vegetable garden and the shearing,
his child's new words
and a wren's nest we'd found.
Never of death:
never of the lengthening shadow
and one man's agony,
the aching hunger for life in his eyes.

There were no portents:
the dogs did not howl all night,
there was no eclipse of the sun
or dark patches on the moon.
Hens continued to lay
and even the day itself
was unexceptional
in its loveliness.

When he left
he soared away from us,
far from the place of his pain
to join the air, the earth, the stars;
to live on only in our hearts;
enshrined in memory
and the smallness of our everydays.

We mourn our loss:
our sorrow bleak, like winter.
He was a son, a brother,
father, lover, friend;
he was Everyman who lived and died
but he was different -
he was ours.

Spring sun warms the soil,
that good rich soil
which earthworms turn.
Wild ducks rest on the brimming dam
and flowers bloom again.
Swallows fly about the eaves
feeding their eager young;
new life burgeons and commands
that we go on.

We hear our laughter echoing
his child's delight,
discovering still newer joys
as summer's pleasures ripen.
We share a love that did not fail
and we find a certain peace.

# LOOKING AT VEINS IN MY FEET

My feet, like me,
are old.
Today they're weary
after a long hike.

I take off boots and socks
and, looking down,
see the veins in my feet
standing proud.

My feet, like me,
are old
but yet remarkable.
These extremities,
formed with the rest of me
in my mother's womb
were pink and perfect
when I was born.
She would have kissed them
and counted toes.

Through 65 summers they've carried me,
mostly uncomplaining.
I've learned to dance on them
and wrap them around the back
of a lover.

Even my callouses
and thickened nails
seem beautiful
as blood pulses through
my knotted veins.

# LINES WRITTEN ON TURNING 64

## remembering Edna St Vincent Millay and Robert Browning

"What lips my lips have kissed, and where, and why...."
she wrote of lovers, lost in time's swirl and sway.
She and I – sisters in experience - share
our half-remembered images which fill the mind,
confounding easy sleep.
Flotsam of experience washes up on beaches of memory
and the ebbing tide sucks and hisses,
as it clutches the departing shore.

The men I loved,
whose bodies I held to mine
as though my life depended on it,
are gone now, faded out, or old, or dead:
I don't remember.
And if I do ever feel a pang of the old hunger,
it passes like a shooting star
and is forgotten.

I am content,
glad to have lived so hungrily, and so long.
Happy to hold the hand of a little child,
appreciating youth and beauty without envy,
looking back without regret.

I have my books.
I have my friends.
I miss the dead ones and I celebrate the living
who "grow old along with me."
And while I no longer recognise
the old woman who looks back from the mirror,
white-haired and lined with life,
I think her face is kind.
I hope I'm right.

# HOLDING ON

She'd do it now, the euthanasia thing,
if it wasn't so deliberate, so absolute,
so permanent.

She should've done it already.
She's got the pills.
It *is* what she wants.
But just not yet.
She wakes to another day
of being washed and changed and fed,
suffering the kindly briskness of those
whose job it is to do such things;
who prop her up so she doesn't look shrunken
when her visitors come;
her staunch and loving family,
who bravely try to hide their horror
at the slow obscenity of her dying.

It *is* what she wants:
to spare them the sight
of blood-soaked, gasping death,
her failed and withered body
attached to tubes and filled with drugs
which no longer touch the pain.

But not today;
not when she can still see the soft camellia
blooming outside the window,
not when she can still hear carefree birds
as they scold and twitter in the eaves,
not when she can still feel cheerful sunlight
reaching her bed,
stirring cold limbs into memories
of past summers filled with living.

They'll soon be here, the nurses say.
She forces her lips into a smile
and hides her palsied hands.

*Darling*, he says, her man, her lover;
her children's father.
He bends to kiss her and she tastes her tears.
Her children touch her hands.
She wants to live.

But she is too tired and soon,
soon it will be time.
But not today.
She's just not ready.
Yet.

# THE SOLDIER

## (after Rupert Brooke)

His forearm, with the burn from his watch
stopped at the moment of the explosion,
was sent back in the coffin
filled with sandbags
to give it body-weight.

The rest of him
was left in Afghanistan
and he was decorated,
posthumously,
back in England
with a medal.

His wife mourns,
his child frets
and cries for Daddy.

And for what?

A corner of a foreign field
that is forever England?

# DEATH OF A GREY MARE

She was born the year I came back to England
and even as I landed would have been
a long-legged filly,
knocking and bumping at her mother's side,
skittering around her meadow
and kicking her heels for love of life.

Dappled grey, she came into my life
as a feisty eight year old mare.
The first time I rode her she bolted three times,
finally throwing me.
But she stayed and looked down
and stood quietly as I remounted.

For eight years we were a partnership
on the hunting field.
Galloping over the moors,
jumping stone walls,
alive and full of joy
until the dusk came
and we would hack home,
wearily, with the hounds.

I loved her.
When I went to the field gate
and called her name,
she would look up, whinny,
then trot to me as an obedient child would.
I would stroke her neck
and play with the tangle
of her beautiful white mane.
"Ladybird", I would whisper.

She broke her leg one day,
and the quick gunshot
was a blessing.
She was not a mare to grow old
and stand by uselessly
as the other hunters
went off to work.

No, far better this way.

But oh, I miss her.

# SPREADING ASHES

The day I spread the third lot of ashes,
my father's,
under a rose bush,
to join two other friends who'd gone before,
three butterflies came
and seemed to watch
my human task.

Perhaps they were three kings,
their souls released,
I mused, as they soared
aloft in sunlight
for one sweet day.

Fragile, beautiful,
haughty and imperious
they kept a distance from me,
and from each other
as they wheeled and dived
and circled.

Then, as if in slow farewell
they dipped their wings
and flew away.

# KITTEN WHISPERING

My friend had lost her kittens:
a mother cat had given birth,
then the following day
had taken her six babies and hidden them
deep in woodland,
spurning the warm house
and the cosy box beside the Aga.
We searched and searched
but found no sign:
the woods too deep, the cat too clever
and the kittens too small
to betray the hiding place.

Six weeks passed.
The Cats' Protection League came
to flush them out:
no-one wanted feral cats in the woodland.
More time passed and three were found.
Had the rest been taken by a fox?

Then one day, as I sat alone,
I heard a tiny cry, a small mewing
from my garden
and saw a streak of tabby under the hedge.

Little and afraid, the kitten watched me warily.
I stood still
and then mewed back to it.
As though we already understood each other,

we mewed and mewed again
until, miraculously,
the kitten came towards me.
Closer and closer it slowly came
as we talked in kitten language:
mew, mew; mew, mew.
I enticed it to my kitchen
without a bribe of food,
just kitten talk.

Then I locked the door behind it,
my first betrayal.

Wildly, it threw itself against the closed door
then hid behind a chair,
hissing if I approached:
"Traitor", it spat,
and scratched when I tried to reach
to grasp it.
I waited for my friend to come,
put out a saucer of warm milk,
then sat quietly, sewing, at my kitchen table.
Time passed: my friend was late,
but still I sat
until I heard a gentle lapping
and all the milk was gone.

My friend arrived with kitten-catching bags
and strong, tough twine.
We pushed the struggling bundle,
biting and scratching with all its small ferocity,
into the bag and tied the knot.

It was my second betrayal that day.

# SCARS

My years are many
and I count my scars:
life etched in ridgelines

The sole of my right foot -
cut by broken glass
as I ran, a barefoot child -
still aches sometimes.
My chin is dimpled
where I crashed my bike
into a gatepost,
knocking myself unconscious
and frightening my father.
The long burn crinkles along my hand
from the time I looked at my reflection
in the new electric iron –
so shiny, so different from the old black ones –
and dropped it.
And my leg is pitted
from an infection
got from scratching under an itchy
Plaster of Paris cast
with a knitting needle.
My childhood,
so unmarked by real tragedy,
is remembered by such small impediments.

A narrow line bisects my thumb –
a legacy of surgery after a skiing fall
in Italy, onto packed ice.
A bare patch on my knee
recalls a skid on a wet tennis court
In Mexico.
And my lip is lopsided
from being split and stitched
after a low-hanging branch
caught me unawares
when galloping my grey mare
through the forest.

There's a belly-button scar
from an ill-omened
IVF attempt,
years ago,
when I'd left it too late anyhow
and was never a good idea;
and the appendix gash
recalls searing pain.

But I'm still here.
And I celebrate my scars.

# THE ARIAS

## Seven ages in musical extremes

**1. Awakening: Un Bel di Vedremo, Madame Butterfly,
Puccini One Perfect Day, Little Heroes**
Bone bleached paddocks
welcome my grandmother's sister
to rural Australia in 1952,
Misty Scotland behind her and, with her,
a sea-trunk full of wonders:
sequinned dresses, feather boas,
silver shoes and a gramophone.
I had grown six years
with only my mother's voice as music,
and now, this miracle.
I sit rapt as she tells the story
of Pinkerton and Butterfly
and let the music pierce me
like beauty and like pain.

Years later
I believed I understood the tears on her cheeks:
an old woman,
spinstered by the Great War.
Did she, too, wait
for a man who never came back?

**2. Young dreams: Triumphal March, Aida, Verdi**
             **Da Doo Ron Ron, The Crystals**

Ten years on
and I've got a crush on the boy next door.
I plan our wedding
and listen to the music that will
take me down the aisle:
a slave girl, ripe for his command.
Bridesmaids in flowing gowns
arrange flowers in my hair
as the rampant masculinity of trumpets
carries me to my love, my destiny.

I spend all day doodling in my school notebook,
entwining our initials together:
dreaming of children
and the house,
small dreams of pillow cases
and casserole dishes.

**3. Getting of wisdom: Va Pensiero, Nabucco, Verdi**
                **Wild World: Cat Stevens**
                **Winter Lady: Leonard Cohen**

London envelops me.
But am I an exile
or prodigal returned?
I feel as though I have come home
although I do not belong.

My hopes soar as I yearn
to take a part.
I am set apart by birth and accent,
poverty stifles me

and the cold chills my bones.
Yet I have made a vow:
I will succeed!

And so I do.

4. **Love: Viene La Sera, Madame Butterfly, Puccini**
      **Oh, What A Night, The Four Seasons**
   And now this joy:
   my mother always said
   I'd know
   when I'd met the right one.
   I did:
   but after a while he seemed wrong,
   and so I tried again,
   and again and again.

   "I love you," I said.
   *Bimba daglia occhi pieni di malia ora sei tutti mia.*
   *Darling, sweetheart, beloved.*

   Like Pinkerton,
   I meant it at the time.

5. **Madness: Ohime! Sorge Il Tremedo Fantasma, Lucia di**
      **Lammemoor, Donizetti**
      **Ruby Tuesday, The Rolling Stones**
   What is this grief
   rising like gorge
   each morning?
   Why can't I get out of bed?
   Why are simple tasks,

like washing my hair,
so insuperable?
Why do I seek oblivion
in sleep or death?
Help me! I beg
the fates
as I soundlessly scream,
"Stop! Stop!"
I am losing my mind
and with it
all my pride.
The blood on the blade
beckons,
the night falls.
I can no longer bear
this suffering.

And then, a miracle
of modern pharmacology
saves me.


**6. Getting on with Things: Canzonetta Sull'Aria, K492,**
**The Marriage of Figaro,**
**Mozart My Life, Billy Joel**
**These Are The Days of our**
**Lives, Queen**

Another twenty years!
I'm growing older,
growing up, maybe, at last.
Who'd've thought it all would be
so satisfying, so complicated
and so much fun?

My music grows along with me
and I find more meanings
in layers which unfurl.
A little wiser, maybe,
I see that beast and beauty
co-exist in all things human.
A little kinder now, I hope,
I seek to find the best.
My simple cup's half-full
to overflowing.

**7. Towards the End: Mild und Liese (Isolde's Liebestod)**
**Tristan and Isolde, Wagner Grane,**
**mein Ross (Brunnhilde's Immolation)**
**Gotterdammerung, Wagner**
**Wondering Where the Lions Are,**
**Bruce Cockburn**

I don't want to spend my twilight
drooling in a nursing home,
subject to care, or lack thereof,
by strangers.

No! Let me go out in a blaze!
Let me choose my time,
face oblivion
in the ecstasy
of controlling
my one last act on earth.

My life is sweet,
and may there be many a good year ahead
when I can walk for miles,
gallop on my horse,
enjoy warmth with loved ones
and listen to my music.

But without an accident,
a heart attack or stroke,
I'd rather take matters
into my own hands
when the time is right
and exit joyfully.

# REGRETS ON SEVEN
# CONTINENTS

## The Cantos

1. **Aspen, Colorado USA 2009**
   The little wooden rabbit, made by hand,
   with less-than-perfect wheels,
   sits at the back of an antique shop
   in the winter playground of celebrities.
   Once this was a silver miner's house
   and the ghostly miner and his child
   hover in corners and sing in chimneys.
   I see him bend by candlelight, whittling wood
   after a day of hard labour in perishing cold
   for poor reward.
   A bowl of gruel, a crust of bread,
   his wife's worried expression,
   remind him of broken dreams
   and winter-withered joy.
   But he carves the toy with love
   and smiles at his sleeping child.
   I leave the shop without a purchase,
   pondering.

2. **Genting Highlands, Malaysia 1983**
   We sang along with Kenny Rogers –
   "The Gambler" on tape
   in the rented car –
   Kuala Lumpur behind us
   and an illusory future ahead.

A runaway couple
with disappointing marriages,
quotidian lives and unfulfilled dreams,
we truly believed that this time
was different
and we beheld the Holy Grail.
Nothing like it, of course.
We got found out
and like the song –
knowing when to hold or to fold,
folded,
and went back to normal life.

### 3. Mt. Erebus, Antarctica 1979

When I heard that so many friends
on Air New Zealand Flight 901
had been killed in the crash
I at first was shocked,
then glad I wasn't one of them;
not rostered on that fateful day
to take sightseers to the Pole,
but safely married in another country.
But they haunted me for years,
that spectral flight crew.
I saw them walking towards me,
their uniforms a splash of colour
in the ghostly white of polar snow
with only cold wind breaking the silence
of incredible stillness
after the impact.
One, a girl, whose body was found embedded
among mangled instruments on the flight deck,
I remembered from a time in Hong Kong,
years before.

She's bought a diamond ring, solitaire,
one carat.
"I'll never marry," she said, presciently,
"but I want a nice diamond."

4. **St. James' Church, Weybridge, Surrey, England 2007**
"Could I use the loo, please?"
I asked the vicar, a kindly woman.
I was there early, for a funeral,
having travelled a long way by train.
"Of course," she smiled at me
and showed the way.
As I washed my hands I saw
on the bench beside the washbasin
a white plastic baby-changer
decorated with tiny teddy-bears.
I thought of the young mothers
who laid their babies here,
smiling as they changed their nappies.
I thought of the baby of the myth
who came to save the world
and felt my atheism rebuked
profoundly.

5. **Annapurna Trek, Nepal 1985**
"Please don't give money to beggars,"
the official leaflet said,
along with advice on not drinking the water
and how to avoid altitude sickness.
"We are trying to build a modern country
with welfare for those in need.
Giving to beggars encourages dependency."

We sterilised our water and drank lots of it
to avoid altitude sickness.
We saw unimaginable mountain peaks
and stars, scattered like daisies
in richly purple nights.

The woman came towards me out of nowhere,
child on hip, another dragging at her ragged skirt.
"Please," she said, and held her hand out.
"Please," again.
I shook my head, remembering the admonition
and walked on.
"Please!" This time she grasped my arm.
I turned to see such desperation,
such despair and hopelessness
as I had never seen
in human eyes before.
I pulled myself away and walked on;
and regretted it ever since.

6. **The Woolshed Dances, NSW Australia 1963**
The lights are dimmed, the saxophone moans
as the gramophone plays the record –
Acker Bilk, "Stranger on the Shore."
You hold me close and my virgin body
responds to the muscular nearness of you.
I am seventeen and you are my first love.
"Don't," Elvis Presley sings,
"don't say don't."
"Don't," I say, and pull away.
Later in the car you kiss me
and desire engulfs
with lambent sweetness.

I push away your hands that seek me.
You drive me home,
a decent boy,
and life takes us in opposite directions.
Years later we meet again,
old and much changed.
But in you I still see the boy
at the woolshed dances
and wonder how it would have worked for us.

## 7. Intercontinental Hotel, Johannesburg, South Africa 1981

I'm awake early,
jetlagged from the long westward flight.
You're asleep so I leave you
in the comfort of the king-sized bed.
I leave a note:
"Gone for a swim. Come down if you wake –
we'll have breakfast."
I put on the five-star bathrobe
and take the lift.
The pool area is deserted,
except for an old black man
dressed in a blue overall, who is sweeping the tiles.
Over the loudspeaker Willie Nelson croons
"Someone to Watch Over Me."
I swim a few laps of lazy breaststroke
then sit at a table to watch the day take shape.
I smile at the sweeper and he smiles back, shyly.
You join me with books and newspapers.
We order breakfast:
two white people waited on
by old black men.

# THE MIRACLES

## -for my mother

You were born in days of miracles:
no foetal scan showed shadowed images
of alien and unfamiliar worlds;
no monitors, no measurements reassured,
just your presence growing under my heart
and the tiny fish-flutter of your kick.

I breathed you into being:
You filled my days with unrelenting clamour
and my sleepless nights with unabated fears:
no certainties assured me, no comfort came
from this wild and wilful child;
even so, I held onto perilous hope.

And now, this blessing in old age:
no secrets hid, you bring me certain peace.
I gave you life, you gave me joy
which I'll take with me, where I go.

We live in days of miracles.